Absolutely Wild

Poems by Dennis Webster

Illustrations by Kim Webster Cunningham

David R. Godine · Publisher · Boston

First published in 2009 by
David R. Godine · Publisher
Post Office Box 450
Jaffrey, New Hampshire 03452
www.godine.com

Design by Carl W. Scarbrough

First Edition
Printed in China

for Scott

THE YAK

A shaggy species is the yak
With hairy front and hairy back.
It isn't very hard to spot him
With hairy top and hairy bottom.
He doesn't mind that he's so shaggy,
If he wore pants he'd like them baggy.
His coat's a frightful mess, and yet
You'd dress as he does, in Tibet.

THE PTARMIGAN

A ptarmigan is a beautiful sight.
In summer she's brown; in winter, white.
Though this little bird has a difficult name
She's very proud of it all the same.
So always remember (I'll be emphatic)
The *p* is silent, as in *pneumatic*.

THE SNAIL

The snail's a funny little fellow
Whose body seems to run on Jell-o.
He slips and slides along the ground
And never makes the slightest sound.
He only has one foot, and so
His speed is very, very slow.
    Still, moving at all is hard, you know,
    When you carry your house wherever you go.

THE SEAGULL

The seagull is a handsome bird
Who looks so spick and span
It's easy to forget that he's
A seashore garbage man.

THE PUFFIN

If you ever meet a puffin,
  Be prepared to be surprised.
He's a stubby little sea-bird
  Whose beak is over-sized.
His body's mostly black and white,
  His manners are quite mild;
The beak's the thing about him
  That is absolutely wild.
He tries to live a modest life
  Like any normal fellow.
But how can he seem average?
  His beak's red, blue and yellow.

THE MOOSE

The massive moose can meet his needs
By munching moss and twigs and weeds.
    He is a solitary fellow;
    All he does is stand and bellow.

A stranger thing you'll never meet:
He's got big knees and bigger feet,
    His nose is huge, his hair is hopeless,
    He smells because his life is soapless.

But when a female wanders by
Her beauty makes him preen and sigh.
    Both look as odd as all their kind;
    It must be true that love is blind.

THE OSTRICH

The ostrich is a splendid bird
    Who's taller than most men.
It seems a little bit absurd
    To call his wife a hen.

This giant can outrun a horse,
    And eats like one, it's said,
So when she lays an egg, of course,
    It's bigger than your head.

GOOD GNUS!

THE GNU

Every good zoo should have a gnu
To help the local papers.
When they have nothing else to do,
Reporters watch their capers.
    And newsmen reach the highest peak
    Of journalistic joy
    When headline type can proudly shriek,
    "Good Gnus – It's a Boy!"

THE SHREW

The shrew's the smallest animal
    That lives upon the earth.
She's rather teeny-tiny from
    The moment of her birth.
There's just one thing that's oversized
    About this little mite;
Her one gigantic feature is a
    Fearsome appetite.
I think it is a blessing that the shrew
    Is made so small;
If shrews grew big as elephants,
    I'm sure they'd eat us all.

THE VULTURE

What can we say about the vulture,
A bird without a shred of culture?
  Her manners aren't among the best;
  She'd be an awful dinner guest.

She eats until her stomach's full.
Her conversation's very dull.
  When asked to sing she'll loudly "crork!"
  She cannot use a knife and fork.

I'd like to find one kindly word
About this bald, untidy bird.
  I had one ready to submit,
  But now I can't remember it.

THE PORCUPINE

The chubby little porcupine's
    A most amazing creature.
She has a pelt that can't be missed
    As her outstanding feature.
I like a little animal
    Whose fur is soft and tickly,
So it's hard to love a porcupine
    Whose back is just plain prickly.

THE ANT

The ant is very active;
She runs around all day.
She scurries yon and hither
And has no time for play.
She never seems to skip or walk,
She's always on the run.
She goes to lots of picnics
But never has much fun.

THE PLATYPUS

The platypus is quite unique.
To start with, up front there's a beak,
   While buried in the cuddly fur
   Of a male's hind leg is a poison spur.

They have webbed feet upon their legs
And the female platypus lays eggs.
   They dine on worms alone, it seems,
   As they swim around Australian streams.

I think that Nature made a blunder,
Then tried to hide it, 'way Down Under.

THE GIRAFFE

An adult giraffe is a towering beast
Who stands over nineteen feet tall.
He weighs about four thousand pounds (or, at least
That's what those who have weighed one recall.)
    People say that his camouflage rating is high
    Because of the spots on his pelt,
    But it seems to me only someone who won't try
    Cannot find a giraffe on the veldt.

THE PENGUIN

The penguin is an awkward bird.
At least, that's what I've always heard.
    He swims and waddles, never flies,
    When other birds act otherwise.

His workday outfit seems so formal
And that, I think, is hardly normal.
    He keeps his egg upon his feet,
    Which doesn't sound so very neat.

Still, I guess the penguin does his best
To raise a child without a nest.
    It's not exactly Paradise
    Living on a slab of ice.

THE GIBBON

Based in the Southeast Asian trees,
The gibbon's life is one of ease.
He's like a little child at play,
Eating and swinging all the day.
All through his life he just relaxes
And never thinks of income taxes.

    He's never heard of a nuclear ban.
    He's free of revolution.
    I sometimes think my fellow man
    Was gypped by evolution.

ABOUT THIS BOOK

During my childhood in Chappaqua, New York, my father Dennis Webster worked as an advertising copywriter in New York City. He had a Masters Degree in Journalism from Columbia University, and was always honing his skills as a writer – as the unofficial "Office Poet" for any special occasion, doing the *New York Times* crossword in ink and making up his own crossword puzzles, and even working at night as a reporter for the local newspaper. When I was about ten he began a series of animal poems to delight me, for by then I was both a voracious reader and a passionate animal lover.

As I grew up and became a more accomplished artist we sometimes dreamed of publishing a book of his poems with my illustrations. And somehow, throughout my many moves as an adult, I always held on to that little folder of typed poems. After majoring in printmaking at Kirkland College in Clinton, New York, I moved to New Hampshire with my husband, Scott, and began a career as an illustrator. I finally realized my father's and my dream of creating our book when I self-published it as a seventy-fifth birthday surprise for him. The text of *Absolutely Wild* consists of sixteen clever poems describing unusual animals, which are enjoyable for both children and adults. The illustrations are hand-colored linoleum block prints, and they and the text are enclosed in decorative borders.

Kim Webster Cunningham